from VICTIM
to SURVIVOR

ROSALYN KERSHAW

Note for Librarians: A cataloguing record for this book is available from Library and Archives Canada at www.collectionscanada.ca/amicus/index-e.html

ISBN 1-4251-0333-2

Printed in Victoria, BC, Canada. Printed on paper with minimum 30% recycled fibre.
Trafford's print shop runs on "green energy" from solar, wind and other environmentally-friendly power sources.

TRAFFORD
PUBLISHING™

Offices in Canada, USA, Ireland and UK

Book sales for North America and international:
Trafford Publishing, 6E–2333 Government St.,
Victoria, BC V8T 4P4 CANADA
phone 250 383 6864 (toll-free 1 888 232 4444)
fax 250 383 6804; email to orders@trafford.com
Book sales in Europe:
Trafford Publishing (UK) Limited, 9 Park End Street, 2nd Floor
Oxford, UK OX1 1HH UNITED KINGDOM
phone +44 (0)1865 722 113 (local rate 0845 230 9601)
facsimile +44 (0)1865 722 868; info.uk@trafford.com
Order online at:
trafford.com/06-2090

10 9 8 7 6 5 4 3 2 1

Introduction

Hi, my name is, Rosalyn Kershaw, I am 28 years
Of age. I am 5ft 2in, 7st 4lbs.

This is my story, every word is true,
However certain names have been changed, due to identity risk.

My aim for this book is to help others to
Become survivors. This book deals
With several issues, some you may have been through
Some perhaps you are still going through.

Let me take you on, through
The journey of my life, my ups and my downs, my successes and
My failures, my gains and my losses.

Please note, this book does contain some strong language,
And also some graphic explanations too.

Thankyou for reading. Thanks to everyone who made it possible
For me to write my book.

Thankyou especially to Jesus for giving me the
Inner strength, patience, and support, and
For keeping me alive to look after my boys
And write my book.

Thankyou to my husband for 9 years of love and support.

Thanks also to our health visitor, Jenny Kolouri
for her excellent support too.

God bless you all.

FROM VICTIM TO SURVIVOR

As far back as I can remember, myself and my 2 sisters, Bethany and Sarah all slept in the same room, and ours was the pink room. Please note that family names have been changed due to identity risks. My 3 other brothers, Philip, Steve and Daniel slept in the blue room in which they had there mattresses on the floor, that's how mother made them sleep. Mother and father slept in the red room. You see the rooms were all coloured to our own specifications. So ours was pink with rainbow bright curtains, the boys was blue with star wars posters, an mother an fathers was just plain deep red.

We lived in Stockport at this time. We were on a road where the people were very upper class and we certainly were not. My father did not get along with our next door neighbours on the left hand side and my mother did not get on with the neighbours on the right hand side. So we were in the middle of a major dispute.

Within the home we were far from a normal family. You could cut the tension and anger within the home with a knife. The home itself took on a life of its own too, as I'll explain further along. If we misbehaved, mother and father would dish the discipline out together, well we would not call it discipline. Mother and fathers idea of discipline for the girls was to be smacked constantly until several hand marks were clearly visible, also used was the slipper, you remember the ones those that had the strange sort of patterns underneath, with a brown sole?, well we were terribly marked with them too, after you had been hit with it, you would have a raised pattern on your leg, bruised with little circles and zigzag markings.

The boy's punishment was more like something from an army camp, they were made to stand against the wall endlessly, or so it felt for hours. In today's day and age this discipline still stands, however it is only meant to be: 1 minute for each year of a child's life, for us it was hours, but as I said the boys got it 10 times worse. Instead of the slipper the boys got the wire straight across the backside, which left them badly marked leaving clear bruising.

We was made to watch each others punishment so that we knew what was coming if we stepped out of line. For normal children, being young was to be free and happy, for us kids however this was not the case, well for 5 of us siblings anyway. The two youngest were the apple of mother and fathers eye and so they should have been too, they were great kids. At times, very rarely, the house would be peaceful, and dare I say it, somewhat happy, however beneath that false joy mother and father both harboured a dark secret which involved me and my twin brothers.

A dark secret that was about to be revealed more and more through our apparent behaviour. The one thing we all enjoyed most of all was being allowed to stay up a little later than usual some nights. Our father would shout "right kids get your blanket's down" we would rush for our blankets and dive on the leather setee, we would all snuggle up together, then the lights would go out. Mother then put on the same thing as every other time, Dracula, my older sister Sarah used to fancy Christopher Lee who played Dracula. Philip, Steve and Daniel, all used to go to bed before us. Then when I drifted off to sleep dad would carry me upstairs to bed, and then he carried Sarah up. We would awake soon after our warm bodies hit the ice cold sheets of our beds.

You see mother and father didn't like to use heating in the house and only put the gas fire on every Sunday after our baths, they was strict on water too. So anyway we were put into our beds and soon awoke shortly after.

The house, as I explained earlier had taken a life of its own on. Each of the 5 of us children all saw something out of the ordinary. Spiritually I mean. We were all positive our home was haunted, we was not the only ones who saw evil things our parents did too.

First Daniel awoke the whole house up several times in the night screaming. He had explained that he had seen a white magician's glove coming towards him and would wrap itself round Daniels neck. The doctor thought the marks on his neck was made by his own hand. Daniel also said he saw demons coming out of the fireplace.

Then my twin brothers, Philip and Steve, they both saw a pulsating blue magnified eye on the wall to which also made a pulsing noise. Then myself and my sister Sarah both saw what we can only describe as three tall black demon type figures standing against the wall, all had started to change, and the other kids at school soon picked up on this, and began to bully me.

They would put their arms in the shape of a cross and say the words "rebound" which to them meant don't come near me. They would all sit well away from me in the class room, and one girl just kept on scratching my arm when she saw me and offered me out for a fight all the time, Ii used to sit all on my own at playtime after dinner and just cry. The other kids they just totally blanked me, they all just ignored and rejected me when I tried to talk to them. I knew I was on my own.

One day, one of the boys in my class came up to me and just booted me in the stomach, I will never forget that feeling I had of desperately trying to gasp for breath, going dizzy just about noticing all of the others laughing at me. Each day at school felt like a year in itself but there wasn't anything at home either. Mother would come to pick us up from school and never failed to bring us a 10 pence mixup. We loved her for that. Then for some reason father started to come too, he used to wear white butterflies on the back of his jeans. And my bullies had a field day with that, they would shout nasty things to him, but because I was just a child I did what any child would do and defend their father. The bullying got 10 times worse for me as a result.

Back home every Saturday mother would send my elder brother and sister to the shop, they would always come back with 2 penny ice-lolly's and rockcake's. The shop owner called Mr. Fox, which was his real name he is dead now and the shop is shut down, Fox knew mother very well and would often allow her to have credit from him. The bill, however mounted up to over £80 pound, mother began to realise that for every time she paid it off she would ask for credit again and had created a vicious circle.

But somehow she still managed to keep things going, our meals each night, every night consisted of either mash and beans or mash and gravy, and really we should of all appreciated this, but one day my twin brothers had a go at mother for it, the reason being is because we all knew, once we had gone to bed, our parents would tuck into a much better meal than us lot ,well mother came storming in the living room, with her face all crumpled up and gritted teeth, she scraped the entire contents over Philip and Steves heads and the plate hit the wall, smashed and sliced both of my brothers ears open. Mother didn't get them to hospital, she patched them up herself with the equipment my brothers had stolen from a hospital, night's before. You were not allowed to mention any incident after it happened, you had to keep it quiet.

Myself and my sister Sarah we used to love going to the newsagents called booths, we would have our pennies ready and would feel real grownup giving the pennies over in exchange for sweets. We would feel even more special if we had a one pound note. By now mother had decided that we could all start to go out. Myself and my sister Sarah used to go to the park and the swimming baths, my little sister Bethany went to the park with a friend, Philip Steve and Daniel used to go off doing things they shouldn't be doing, the police was for ever round at the house.

At school myself and my sister Sarah had started to nick off, we would go down to the river and just chill out, they were the good moments, well until the head teacher caught us that is, then it was back to school and bullied again. Sarah wasn't bullied much, she would have one or two of them calling her bent ear, her ear was just slightly misshaped, but mother took her to hospital to get it fixed. Or she would be called scrubber, because they knew that we wasn't upper-class like them, in fact we was rather poor in comparison to them, but Sarah had a lot more friends than me, certainly in school and out of school also, she was quite popular.

Myself and Sarah also loved the weekends. we would get a beeline bus into town from the bus stop outside our house, and we would head straight off to Woolworth's in Stockport, we would wait until the security guards were out of view and cram pack a pick n mix bag full of sweets then leg it back on the bus and back home, we would then give them to mother. We did get caught a couple of times, but the policeman who caught us knew the family well, he was nicknamed Spike, he would caution us and let us go.

On the Sunday, this day was quite different to the rest, as me and Sarah was in the choir at St, Mary's church. We used to get a £50 cheque every month, standing together. The rest I saw I am quite sure you wouldn't believe but I am going to tell you anyway. I also saw my big massive yellow teddy walk across the room towards myself and my sister. You would hear a kind of loud humming noise just before all these things happened. We all had heard the same strange noise just beforehand.

Mother apparently saw her mother our grandma in a rocking chair just rocking back and forth, grandma died the year I was born. Father used to occasionally sleep on the landing and said he distinctively remembers a little girl dressed all in white cross over his bed and vanish into the next room, some sceptics would try to make some sort of logical sense out of what we all saw, like we all started to see things very similar to the discipline we was receiving, or we was seeing our own trauma within, or father saw a little girl because that's what he wanted to see, and if that's the case, then what the hell was the teddy doing walking? What logical sense is there for that?. We were not on drugs, well not yet anyway.

Every night about midnight father would take the family dog "Rusty" for a walk. He was so paranoid that someone was about to break in, he would tie one end of a long wire to mothers wrist and the other end he tucked under the mat outside the back door, he would be gone for a good couple of hours. When he returned from his walk in the woods he would give 1-2-3 tugs on the end of the wire, still attached to mothers wrist, that way she would know it was father, and not some psychopath.

Some nights he would take myself my elder sister and twin brothers with him for a walk to the woods. It was really scary but we loved it Father used to have a flask of tea made with marvel milk and a packet of polo mints. After quite some time we would all rest on a log and have a cup of fathers tea, it was so sweet and tasty, then followed by a polo mint we would all head off back home. Almost every day was the same old routines and punishment's, so going to the woods was a really big thing to us.

We was still very young then, I was about 7ish Sarah was about 9ish Philip was 11ish as was his twin Steve, and Daniel was about 13. The youngest Bethany she was about 5 years old and was asleep before the rest of us. Mikey our little brother was not long just born. He would have been about 8 months old.

Our wonderful walks with father in the woods at night was about to come to an end. When I got to my birthday things within the family home went from bad to worse. My father had started to get me up in the middle of the night and would take me downstairs, he often said he just wanted a chat, but when we sat down on the settee his intentions became clear. My father had started to sexually abuse me. He made me do things to him and he did things to me.

Mother was in bed. Night after night after night my father continued to abuse me if I said "no" I would have been punished for it, the next day he would of gone into a foul mood and give me more punishment than usual. He would also take it out on my mother. My brothers only recently told me of the pain and suffering they encountered at the hands of mother as a direct result of father taking it out on her. My brothers confessed that mother used to beat them both to the extent that they would inevitably pass out. She strangled them and bit them on their heads, she would make their noses bleed after smacking there heads off the wall. My brothers were quite small for their age, they were slow developers. You could see that they were scared to death of mother but at that time nobody knew what was going on with the other, it was all done in secret. I do remember seeing lumps on their heads and remember their nose bleeds.

They also remember when I kept asking mother for some cream saying I was sore between my legs. This is the only things we remember about each others suffering that wasn't right, the rest came out recently.

Father by now had told me to stop asking mother for the cream, and that he would give it to me. He had also started to give valium to help me to relax, before he would start abusing me. Now however, he had taken things a step further, he had started to attempt to penetrate me, he would attempt it bit by bit every night, I would go back to bed bleeding and sore. For mother to awaken me in the morning was murder for her, as I was just so tired and in pain. But I had to get up to attend school. School was another thing I dreaded because you see, by now I had started to feel much older than the other kids and everything about me had changed. The other kids picked up on this and had begun to bully me every day.

Myself and my sister used to love attending the church choir and we got a bonus of £50 just for doing what we liked to do and that was singing. I don't know maybe in some innocent way we all thought by giving mother things would make her happier, lets face it, weather your being hurt by your parents or not, what child does not want to please its parents.

We loved the choir it was serious, but fun too, well one day Sarah and myself couldn't stop giggling in the service and when it was over we both got kicked out.

At the swimming baths we had met 3 young lads; they took us to their uncle's to introduce us. Little did we know that their uncle was also a child molester. He used to make his own home made beer to which we all drank, their Uncle Ron, who is also dead now, touched me and Sarah several times, and one day the youngest of the lads confessed to me that his uncle was touching him too there was nothing I could do, however we went there more and more as I desperately tried to protect this lad, I stayed with him and became his shadow. And for a time it worked.

Back home, it was the night time I feared the most, I knew that once I fell asleep father would quietly enter our room and wake me up, I hated it, I would lie there still, my heart would be pounding, I dreaded it. I wanted to talk to my brothers about it because I trusted them. But at night they would have a bolt on their door so they couldn't get out. The toilet was out of the question, they had to hang on till the morning, even if they was bursting.

Some nights we would all play up, bouncing on the beds and giggling and shouting to each other through our locked doors. You could hear mother creeping up the stairs and you would dive into bed and say "it wasn't me", or pretend to be asleep.

There was one room in the house we all feared the most, it was the front room, it was empty with no carpet just a black hard floor, mother and father would keep the black rubbish bags full up in there ready to be taken out days later. It was also the room our dog rusty was allowed to poo and wee in, in the daytime. Father was far too paranoid to take the dog out in the daytime. He didn't just leave the room with the dog poo all over the floor, he did clean it and disinfect it, but the fact was, we all knew about it.

This was night time's punishment room. Your mattress

would be thrown on the cold hard floor and you was made to sleep in there, in the pitch black of the darkness. You have to try to imagine it, the front room was pitch black, it stunk of disinfectant, there was full rubbish bags in the corner of the room, the darkness was scary enough whilst your eyes adjusted to the dark, all at the same time as knowing about the weird things that was going on in the house around you.

While in there the black bags used to make noises by themselves and shadows would cross over the walls, it was so frightening and there was an overwhelming feeling of another presence in there, an evil presence. I was only in there 5 minutes and I would scream "mother let me out please I am sorry". But nothing, you were locked in. If you remained quiet for a few hours there was a possibility that you would be allowed out. That room was terrifying.

Myself and Sarah had started to share a bed together, because we were so scared of all the weird things going on in the house. Our sleeping together didn't stop father continuously waking me up in the early hours. I dreaded every night Sarah didn't wake up when father came in, she was a heavy sleeper. Morning was such a relief for me, although it was no escape for me, as I had to face the kids at school then.

Philip, Steve and Daniel had started to get into serious trouble. They were coming home with burns all over their hands from lighting fires, and they had begun robbing from factory's and places like that. The police were around almost every night.

One night they brought home lots of sweets they stole from a factory, this was great as we got to feast out, but not so great for mother. One day a woman came round, we didn't know who she was; mother said she was a social worker. We did not know what one of them was. Mother explained to us that our brothers Philip, Steve and Daniel all had to go into voluntary care. Voluntary care meant they could visit whenever they liked and still have all their freedom. They visited quite a lot and would bring home biscuits and bits of food for us all. Hugging them and saying goodbye was really hard but especially for mother. Myself and Sarah had started to act up even more; we used to swing off the ceiling lights, and jump off from really high heights.

Well one day the light came away from the ceiling after we swung on it, and oh boy was we in serious trouble. We were whacked so hard on the backside several tunes we found it hard to sit down, and then we had to face the wall for hours on end. Another good thing I can remember was that father had made a little hole in the wood of the stairs and we used to put pennies and so on down this slot, I am sure its still there to this day. There was no way of getting to it without ripping up the stairs.

One day on the park myself and Sarah had met two guys older than us. One had a car the other had a motorbike. I began a relationship with the one with the motorbike called Chris, and Sarah began a relationship with the other one called Terry. We had started sexual relations with them, but you see I was not a virgin anyway as my father took that. But Sarah was and she said she will never forget her first time, I however was not allowed that pleasure of a first time, but I did feel the first time crush.

My boyfriend's father was our next door neighbour, the ones my father hated, so we had to keep it pretty much a secret. Some night's father's brothers would come round. Mother was in debt apparently with a catalogue that our uncle was running. We knew nothing of this at the time. At one point our Uncle Eric came round, he is also dead now, I think he must have been having problems with his wife who was a certified schitzophrenic.

Our father told him to sleep on the landing. I loved to chat with him. When he left, a few days later, his wife turned up at our house wielding a knife and threatening our parents. Mother got on the phone to someone and an ambulance came to pick her up.

One day, when our youngest brother Mikey was about 2 years old we all went to our Auntie and Uncles house this was mother's side of the family. We loved it there, myself and Sarah used to let our hair down and just dance and dance to maddonna. We loved it, but we only ever went there just the once. We was really glad that they videoed it, I still have the video now years on.

One night father got me up in the early hours of the morning, as he always did, however this time it was different. Father hugged me and broke down crying, I asked him what was wrong and then he told me. "You and Sarah are going into care but it will not be voluntary, it will be an award of court". I cried my eyes out, I didn't want to go away. Father explained that being an award of court was different from voluntary care, in an award of court the judge makes all the decisions, and I may not be able to see my parents much.

I didn't wait for father to say another word, I shot upstairs and woke Sarah up and told her what was going to happen to us, Sarah broke down too And after talking all night, we both came up with our own plan. The next day we leapt out of the window with a bottle of cider in our hands and broke into this mans house that we knew. This man liked me and Sarah for all the wrong reasons "typical" he used to give us both money for dancing in front of him. He wasn't in at this point. We both drank half a bottle of cider each, when all of a sudden we heard cars screeching outside. We looked out of the window and we saw 3 police cars and several social workers, we made a run for it, tipsy the ground beneath us felt as if it was moving, we felt like we was running really fast, but in fact we was not. The police caught up with us and restrained us and placed us into separate cars. We were devestated, I cried for mother, my heart was breaking, "I want my mummy I would cry." Sarah was crying too.

After about half an hours driving we came to this house called otter burn children's home. We were sent straight to our bedroom where we was put in together which we was really glad of. We had to remain in there till we sobered up. After a heavy sleep "you can imagine" we both woke up, we didn't even know where we was, and could only vaguely remember what happened. So there we were stood at the bedroom door. We were scared stiff, and missing mother like crazy. We opened the bedroom door and saw a lad and a girl race down the stairs shouting "breakfast" we reluctantly made our way down the stairs gripping on to one another's hand.

A woman saw us and asked us to come into the office. She was really nice; we thought we were going to be punished for something. But no all she said was "welcome to otter burn children's home, my name is Bab's" and explained the new rules and punishments to us. The new rules were alien to us, you had to ask to use the toilet, always tell the staff where you were going and so on. Pocket money was great though, we got £15, and I think it was £15 every fortnight.

We loved otter burn it was great, except we still missed home like mad though I didn't miss the punishments or the abuse I suffered. I was quite glad to be getting undisturbed nights sleep. Sarah and I used to go out at night with the lads drinking cider, we didn't have sex or anything like that, we was just mates that all, but we still enjoyed it. However the staff was becoming increasingly concerned about our behaviour.

One day they called myself and Sarah into the office and told us that we were both about to be fostered out, but not together. "No no" we cried we only had each other left. Mother came up to visit and tried to calm us down, but I cried even more because I had to say goodbye to mother too. In fact it wasn't a quick goodbye, the social workers dragged me away from mother, I was screaming and crying so bad my heart was breaking, I ran to Sarah and we wrapped our arms around each other and wouldn't let go. We were literally prized apart by the social workers. Sarah went first into the social workers car and left. Then I went second and left.

Sarah got on with her foster parents, I didn't. My foster father kept throwing ice cold water over me for saying I hated him and wanted to go home, he gritted his teeth at me just like mother used to. I didn't stay there, I kept running away and going back home to mother and father. I would only be there about 2 hours and the police would drag me back to the foster carers. The care system is supposed to be the place you would feel safe, but not for me. The foster parents would hate me every time I was brought back telling me to "get out of their sight."

Meanwhile Sarah was getting along with her foster carers but she was dramatically changing, she started to act like a little girl. She would constantly seek her carer's attention and praise. She told them she didn't want to see me anymore. Although I believe this was their idea not Sarah's. I was so upset when I was told, I completely went off the rails. Back and forth every day to my parents I would go, and the police brought me back every time too.

Until one day when I had been there just two weeks, they

had enough of me. They told me they had rang the social worker and she was coming to pick me up and take me to another placement, "well no way I thought", and off I went again back to my parents home. This time was different, this time I knew something wasn't right, the police pulled up in a riot van, and they were very heavy handed with me, and they bruised my wrists as they pushed me in the back of the van. I could hear mother and father shouting "what the hell is going on". I was in floods of tears once again. The police van set off. I was in the back and could not see where we was going. It felt like we was driving for ever when suddenly the van ground to a halt, Ii could hear voices outside, then the van doors swung open and they dragged me out and handcuffed me, so I couldn't run. Felt like a bleeding criminal, I hadn't done a damn thing wrong.

Anyway a fattish sort of man appeared at the door of this building which was called "Belmont observation and assessment unit" as he came to the door, I could of sworn he opened about 5 or 6 locks. "Is this a bloody prison" I thought." What could I have done to deserve this"? All was about to become clear. The staff said I was there for constantly absconding and returning to my parent's home, where he said the social services had suspected child abuse done to me, I had no idea they knew about this.

There were three units in Belmont, there was the girls unit, which is the one I was on, and this unit was the secure unit, more like a prison. You couldn't go out and were punished for stepping out of line. Then you had the link unit, this was an open unit where you could go out and do what you liked, to an extent. Then there was the boys unit, this was both open and closed depending on how good you were. It consisted of all males, as was the girls unit, all girls. The fact that the unit I was on was secure, did not stop me from trying to escape. I would go round to the front office knowing that the door was left open quite a lot, and I would make a run for it, but often got caught.

When you did get caught, or brought back by the police, if you managed to succeed, the punishment of two weeks worth of sanctions was dished out. The punishment was, you were made to wax down every door on the unit, over and over again, and for the rest of the time you were sat at a little table alone and made to face the wall. I never got on with the girls in my unit; I often got bullied by them too. You see the girls were a lot older than me and had resided there longer, so as you know the new one always gets it.

After repeated attempts and successes of absconding I finally started to calm down. It was getting on past a year that I had been there. When one day the my social worker told me they was going to stop my father from visiting me, well, that's the worst thing they could of done. At this stage all my good work of trying to calm down just went completely out of the window I had started to self harm; it began with scratches then got deeper and deeper. I would use anything I could get my hands on, from staples to smashed crockery. You see at night, we was all locked in our rooms, "like I said it was like a prison." That for me was the perfect opportunity to cut myself, I would start on my arms then my legs then my neck, the worst was on my arms.

One night while I was asleep I heard a tapping noise at the window. As I went to the window I was shocked and amazed to see my twin brothers standing there, rushing to unscrew the windows. They got me out and we legged it through the gap in the fence they had cut. They had to unscrew the windows you see, because they would only open, normally a couple of inches, so you was lucky if you could get your hand through. Anyway my twin brothers Philip and Steve got me out; we ran through the woods and finally ended up at mother and fathers house.

The staff wouldn't have found out, because they never did check on us in the night. There I was standing in front of my parents, so relieved to see them. Father said "Rosalyn please don't take me to court for what I did to you" I promised father that I would never do that. We were all crying and father kept saying he was sorry for all he had done to me. I told him that I had forgiven him. Father had seen my arms and the cuts on them, and for some reason he attempted to self harm too, he had cut a massive cross into his chest, apparently, someone knocked on the door, could have been the police, and saw a towel full of blood, I remember mother coming to see me and told me about it a couple of days later. I was now just 10, nearly 11 years old.

Saying goodbye was the hardest thing, as my brothers had to get me back before the staff unlocked the doors in the morning. Once again I found my heart being shattered and broken. We walked back slowly to Belmont as we chattered along the way. When we got there I climbed in the window, and my brothers screwed it back up again. I said my goodbyes through the tiny gap.

Next day as per usual we all sat at the table for breakfast and this one girl, who I did not get on with, started to have a go at me for no reason what so ever. She said to me, when her father visited I had to make him a cup of tea or she was going to "kick my fucking head in" so frightened, I had to do as she told me. She was a big girl. Her father arrived with her mother, and I made them all a cuppa.

This went on visit after visit. Her father was actually her step father. One day her step father asked me to kiss him, when we were left in the visiting room alone, while Melanie showed her mother her room. I didn't know how to say no to him, and he was a rather big man. So he kissed me. And on every visit when I took a cuppa in to them all, he kept on whispering messages to me, I felt really uncomfortable.

In my life, things were starting to go from bad to worst. My self harming got so deep I was taken to the infirmary for stitches. This went on again and again. I had now been in Belmont for 2 and a half years and I was about 12 nearly 13 years old. Belmont got onto the phone to the social workers and told them that I was out of control and they could no longer handle me. I was immediately shipped off to a place called Prestwich, I was only in there 1 month.

In that time I was assessed for mental illness, because of the self harming. Well I even managed to cut myself there, even though Prestwich was more secure than Belmont was. The fencing had barb wire round them, and all the doors were made of steel, and constantly locked. Here you could not escape. I was the only female on the unit at this point. There was a member of staff who worked there called Malcolm who had started to abuse me. I smoked you see, and was not allowed to in this unit, so Malcolm used to make a deal with me. He would say "I'll flick the ciggy in the corner and when I'm done, you go and get it" he then used to crawl under the ping pong table and do things to my private parts while under there.

I hated it and was so scared when he was on night duty where the staff sleeps in the unit. I was forever being restrained, I was not allowed to see my mother or father, and I would break down crying every day. Malcolm was on duty about 8-10 times while I was there and each time he did what he did, and got away with it. After two weeks of living there, another girl arrived so I got to chat with another female, at least for the final two weeks anyway. Then came the last week and I was told that

I would be shipped off to an emergency placement when the last week was up, I was to be taken all the way from Manchester to Peterbourgh.

The ride there was endless, it seemed to go on for ever. I didn't have a drink or nothing all the way. Finally after 3 hours driving we arrived at Salters secure unit. It was very much like Prestwich but without the psychiatric doctors. It was again so secure you could not possibly escape. I was not allowed to see mother here either. It had been weeks since I had seen her.

I was only in Salters for a week and each day was a living hell. One girl set fire to her mattress and blamed me for it. Another girl barricaded herself in her bedroom and we all lost our privileges because of it. The staff would sometimes become violent, and push you up against the wall with your arm up your back saying "open your flicking mouth again I'ill kill you do you understand?" again "do you understand?" louder this time, crying my eyes out, shaking, I would simply reply "yes yes I understand". I was so glad when the social worker said I was to be moved that day, a week on.

This time I was to be moved to Briarshey secure unit in Liverpool, the unit I was on was called Orchard house, this was the secure area. It was an all female unit. Here I quite liked it. The girls were great, I managed to make one really good friend called Tanya we used to have a really good laugh, and we was forever in trouble, being restrained, and locked in our rooms. This place is where my self harming got worse. I was quite used to their local hospital by now, and they were quite used to me too.

I spent two years in this unit and by now I was so institutionalised, I was too frightened to face the outside world. Though my self harm became worse here, I still classed it as the best secure unit I had been in. Mother was allowed to visit me here too, but I hated saying goodbye to her, knowing we was not going to see each other for another 2-3 weeks, I guess this was the very reason my self harming became twice as bad.

One day the staff took us to Red bank school for swimming. You see you could only go out in orchard house if you had built up enough good points up on your chart system, so those of us that did we would be taken swimming. My friend and I called Rachel, had made a plan to run away. We managed to get through the shower windows in the girl's area and we succeeded. We ran for our lives until we were dehydrated and our throats and chests were killing us. As we stopped we noticed a lad doing a runner too, so we all went together, as he knew where he was going.

We all got to this old house that was hardly lived in by this other lad. One of them said, after two days being on the run, that he had some magic mushrooms. We all ate them and man I'll tell you, I would never do it again. I hallucinated into thinking I was an orange, and with a razor blade I tried to peel myself. I was quite badly cut and didn't realise it was blood because while tripping it just looked like juice coming out of the orange. "Mad I know" my friend said she saw the plants dancing and singing, and we both saw the carpet looking like it was breathing. Well we would never take them again. I patched my own arms up after the mushrooms had worn off, as I found myself in a small pool of blood.

Anyway after three days of being on the run, we got caught, the lad we had gone on the run with, we had begun a relationship, except I knew full well that he was up in court the next day, after saying goodbye to him, myself and Rachel went for a walk, and got caught on a main road by the police. We first ended up spending hours in a police cell before being dragged back to orchard house. We wasn't allowed out for weeks, and they stopped two of my visits with my mother. I was so upset, stopping my visits was the worst punishment for me, I just sobbed and sobbed. When my mother was finally allowed to visit she came with bad news. She told me that father had taken a serious overdose of tablets and was on a life support machine. I was locked up, I couldn't do anything for goodness sake. I begged the staff to "please let me out to see him" but they wouldn't let me. I began to kick off because they raised their voices at mother saying "she should not have told me". I tried to push the staff away from mother and they dragged me to my room, while the other manhandled mother and pushed her out of the front door, I was fuming I had hidden a piece of crockery in mly bandage and began slicing at my arms, crying my eyes out; I just didn't care any more. Slash after slash I made. The bed was now becoming full of blood I just lay down and hoped I would bleed to death. However that wasn't the case the staff checked on me through my locked door, and saw splashes of blood all over the yellow carpet.

They unlocked the door and dragged me to the office, where the blood was now congealing and clotting but the wounds however stayed pretty much open. They didn't take me to hospital because they knew I would just rip the stitches out. My heart was just broken, I was numb. If I couldn't get my hands on broken glass or crockery, I would go and get staples out of magazines, and shove them deep into the cut's, this episode however, did need hospital treatment. They had to operate on my arm to get the staples out, as on the xray, they were very close to the bone. And if I couldn't get hold of these any more, I would rip strips off the mattress and, tighten them round my neck till

I went blue, but the staff always managed to check on me just in time. They would just cut the strip off my neck. If you were caught self harming, the entire contents of your bedroom, including bed, would be taken from you and you were made to sleep on the floor.

This is pretty much how things always were in Briarshey. We had our laughs, myself and a few others, but there was always the underlying pain in my heart of missing my parents. I had already spoken up about the abuse I suffered from father, I had spoken out at Belmont, I had spoken to a psychologist while I was there. She used to give me cigarettes in return for information.

Anyway two years on into Briarshey placement, the staff told me that a high court judge in London had said that "the social services had to put me in an open unit as they feared I was to become institutionalised, I already was, as they were about to find out. On the last day of my stay, a member of staff walked me to the front door and unlocked it. After saying my goodbyes to my friends in there, I stepped outside. Fear raced through my entire body, I sweated, and went pale. "No" I cried, tears streaming down my face "I don't want to go please don't make me go" my heart was racing ten to the dozen as the staff forced me into the car and locked all the doors.

From here I was to be taken to Blackburn, I can't remember the name of this children's home. However the new placement was an open unit, and it took me days to get used to it. When I finally did get used to it, I kept on going to the field where there was a horse that I used to give an apple to. One day I saw the youngest boy in the home being restrained. I just lost it; I grabbed the staff and pulled them off this boy shouting at them "to leave him alone". I was only there for about 9 days and they kicked me out for interfering. The social worker took me all the way back to Belmont. Where, once again I ran off to see my mother and father.

After about a week, the authorities gave up on me, and allowed me to return home to my mother. So I had been in care 4 and a half years, I was 14 nearly 15 when I came out. My dates are all screwed up, I am sorry. By this time, mother now lived in Reddish, Stockport, and father had a flat called Mount pleasant in hazel grove, Stockport. Father was not allowed near mother as the visits to my little brother and sister, Mikey and Bethany would of been stopped. Mikey and Bethany were taken off mother when I was in Belmont, and they were both placed with foster parents.

At home back with my mother, I was told that my brothers had been sent to prison for theft. And she explained about father too, except father didn't stick to the rules, he stayed with mother anyway and would hide if anyone came round. I was still self harming even at home, as now it had become a habit, a way of releasing emotions. I could see when I got home, just how depressed my parents had become since they lost my little brother and sister, after they was taken into care. Belmont had become an open unit by now and was being refurbished. I kept on going back to say hello to one or two of the staff, and I would sneak into the kitchen, and then I would fill carrier bags full of food for mother, I thought it would cheer her up. It did, for perhaps all of half an hour, then she would become really down again.

Mother and father no longer slept in the bedroom of the new house in Reddish, they had begun to sleep on the floor in the living room, well father did, mother had the settee besides him. I watched them both day after day, barely able to exist. One day I started to blame myself for it all. I went to the social services building in the dead of night, and attempted to burn it down.

I hated them, I despised them, and, I didn't get far. All I managed to do was scorch the front door. The police arrived and this
police man remembered me from years back He took me to the
police station but, I wasn't arrested. You see I was still only 14
years old, but I am not any good at dates at all, so please forgive
me. Everything happened so close together you see. I told the
policeman everything that had happened since the day I got
taken away from home, he just seemed to be more concerned
with the fact that my father was still around, though I never told
him that he was still living with mother. I could see he had tears
in his eyes, then told me he was taking me back to my mother,
I feared father might be there and get caught, but I knew he
would hide just in time. It was rather funny seeing father dive
out of bed, and into the cupboard every time the door went, he
tried to make me laugh by pulling funny faces through a gap in
the cupboard door.

Anyway the policeman didn't repeat anything I said to
mother, to my relief, otherwise I would of got the brunt end
of it. After a few days of being back home, I decided to go for
a long walk in the rain, I had always liked that even as a child.
This time though, I wasn't just going for a walk. By watching
my parents trying to give up on life, gave me no incentive to
live either. I piled my pocket full of antidepressants that I had got
from my doctor, and I went to the building of the social services.
I hid behind all the great big bins. Handful by handful I popped
them in my mouth and swallowed them with bottled water, I
remember walking to the fences near Reddish sports field. The
next thing I knew I was outside my parent's front door, I have
no idea how I got there. Mother didn't ring an ambulance, she
dealt with things herself. When in the evening I came round,
mother told me how she dealt with me. She told me she had put

salty water in my mouth, then put her fingers down my throat to make me sick, she did this several times then kept an eye on my pulse rate. I should have been dead, I am sure I managed to take over 60 pills, before passing out. But I believe that, with mothers help god kept me alive.

The next morning about 3:00 am, I stumbled into the kitchen to get a drink, this I am about to tell you is as the rest of my story, no word of lie. I stumbled into the kitchen, and the door suddenly slammed behind me. I leant over the stove to get my cup on the other side, I know, I did not turn on the rings on the stove. All of a sudden my whole chest was on fire, though I felt nothing, no pain at all, I managed to scream just loud enough, and both my parents forced the door open, and put the fire around my chest out. Again mother dealt with it alone with father. She took off my burnt clothing to reveal a ring off the stove around my right breast which had burnt deep into my breast. And I had other blistered burns surrounding it.

Mother put an ice cold towel over my chest and lay me down on the settee. Father gave me some extremely strong painkillers, as by now I had started to feel the burning pain, it was agony. The painkillers really helped. I ended up with a bandage with Vaseline smothered all over it, going right round my chest. "Mothers home made remedy".

Whilst on a visit to the social worker, I was told that a girl I resided with in Belmont, was living just round the corner. It was my arched enemy; Melanie. I decided to go and see her and put a few things right. When I got there she seemed to be really nice to me, as we hadn't seen each other since my first stay in Belmont. Her stepfather Brian was there, I met her mother again too. Melanie started to ask me about what had happened since Belmont. Most of it I could not tell her, she wouldn't understand. I just tried to tell her the good bits. Her stepfather was still trying to make advances towards me, and one night walked me home. He asked if he could see me the next day, and I said "ok". .Mother allowed him in, and we went upstairs.

Brian was the kind of guy who didn't take no for an answer. He came onto me and then forced his way, I said "I wasn't ready" but he said "you'll be fine". And with that he had sex with me, I had to pretend to enjoy it. This went on day after day week after week. I was so sore, so young, and so vulnerable. As I said he wouldn't take no for an answer.

One day he told me that he was due in court for ringing cars, stealing them, and asked me to go with him. The case was being held in the crown court in Manchester. By now I had developed a lot of feelings for him, I didn't know any better, and this kind of thing had been going on all my life. So there we was, we went on the bus to the crown court. The solicitor told him to plead guilty; I had a bad feeling about all this. There he was up in the dock and pleaded guilty, the judge sentenced him to, 2 years imprisonment into Strangeways.

Brian had left his wife for me, he was 36 years old, and I was still 14, there I was stuck all alone in Manchester after Brian was sent down, I didn't have a clue which bus to get on or anything, and I was in floods of tears. The police helped me to get home after I had explained everything to them. Brian often sent me visiting orders from prison and my mother would come with me.

One day I got so depressed, I cut my arm really badly, so deep I had to go to the infirmary as my bone was showing through. The nurses rushed me straight through to the side ward for stitches, while I was sat there, a porter came in and said "he knew my sister Sarah" When I asked him where she was, he told me she was in Stepping hill hospital psychiatric ward.

I couldn't believe it. He then asked me "did I want to go for a drink with him after work" and I said "ok". When he finished work, he took me to a pub in Edgily, Stockport. He bought me a half pint of cider. I became tipsy very quickly. I told him I was 14, and he said it was ok. After my second half, I can't remember much. I can remember being near his flat and that's it, oh and being violently sick. Then the next thing I remember was waking up in his single bed with him, and I was naked, he had his arm round me I asked him if we had sex and he said "yes", I said I didn't remember, but he called me a liar. He said that now we had sex, I had to move in with him but I was not allowed to tell anyone. I still didn't get my stuff together to move in with him, I didn't want to leave my mother.

Anyway he came home from work drunk. He had been to the pub after work. He shouted at me and said "wheres your fucking gear", and with that he dragged me by my hair and threw me on the bed and locked me in his room. I just cried, not because he hurt me, but because I wanted my mother. He unlocked the door, and made me ring my mother to tell her I was ok. Mother knew something wasn't right. I told Joe the porter, that I needed to visit mother and to get my stuff together. I raced home and told mother everything; father was there and said he was going to kill him. I desperately tried to calm father down, as I knew among all the tablets in his bag he also carried a hammer around with him.

Father never let the bag out of his sight; I knew its contents because he showed me. It contained hundreds of different sorts of tablets, a freshly made flask as that's how he had his drinks of tea, he also had a hammer and some pornographic magazines in there. One day, father had taken all the tablets out and neatly placed them into three piles, this is what he said "this section is your's Rosalyn, this section is your mother's, and this section is mine" I didn't know what he was talking about at first, until he said "very soon Rosalyn all three of us are going to take our lives together" I was shocked, but glad in a way, because I had nothing and felt so used and hurt.

Anyway I got my stuff together, the bit I had anyway, and got a taxi back to Joes flat. He acted all, "oh I am glad to see you, I love you so much, I can't live without you." When he had a drink however he turned into jackal and Hyde. He would hit me and drag me by my hair across the room, and tell me I was pretty but he was going to rearrange my face. I was so scared of him.

Day after day it was like this, but only after he drank alcohol. After the first time he had sex with me, it rarely happened after that, with Joe it was all about a power trip, not sex, I was still 14. He used to come home from work and ask where his tea was. So I had to make it for him. It was summer now, Brian had been in prison for about 10 weeks, and I was made by Joe to end the relationship with Brian while he was in prison. The visits got stopped anyway because the governor found out my age.

One night he had taken me out for a drink again, and I was unusually sick after just one mouthful. I told Joe I wanted to go home. He stayed, and I dreaded the thought of him coming home, so I did not stick around, I went straight home to mother and told her about being sick, and she said she thought I may be pregnant "what" I said, I am too young. Well mother bought 2 pregnancy tests the next day, and to my surprise both were positive.

Joe rang mother to ask where I was, and father got on the phone and said "ring here again or touch my daughter again, I will break your fucking legs" with that he slammed the phone down. There was no way I could go back now, Joe would have killed me, so I had to leave all my stuff there.

As time went on I began to show more and more, and then guess what? Yes you guessed it, the social services found out. They didn't seem to care, but this was all a front, as I was to find out upon giving birth. I had decided to get my life together for the baby's sake. I was so happy. I was a budding young mother to be, really chuffed. Christmas was soon upon us, and mother didn't celebrate any more because my little brother and sister wasn't there. So in my innocence, I had uprooted a little tree from the garden, and put tinsel all over it, and with the few pence I had, I bought some decorations to hang up. "What a good job I have done" I thought.

By now I was nearly 15 and 6 months pregnant. I had not self harmed for 6 months, and was getting my life back on track. Mother was acting strange, and she appeared really angry, she got off the couch, crying her eyes out, she shouted "I have lost my fucking kids, I don't want these fucking decorations up" and she ripped the whole lot down, and broke up the little tree I made. I just ran upstairs in floods of tears. Mother came up about an hour or two later, and said she was sorry, and that she was missing Mikey and Bethany. I said "but mum I am your daughter too", but she just said sorry again, and walked off. I went into the living room and sat besides her on the settee, very calmly Ii asked her "do you blame me for what happened between me and father"?, and do you blame me for my little brother and sister being taken away?" To the question about father she replied "no" but to the question about my brother and sister, she said she did blame me. I of course carried this guilt around with me.

Christmas passed, and spring was upon us. I was now 15

years old. I had got all the babies stuff ready, the cot, the pram, the baby bath, everything I could possibly think of, I was so looking forward to the baby's birth. Every day I would say a little prayer over my baby for god to protect her. I knew the baby was a she because of the scans, I had attended every one and did every thing right. I really tried to look after myself.

One night, I was sat next to mother and laughing and joking with her, when a flood of water released beneath me and overwhelming pain seared through my stomach contracting every few minutes. Mother said I was in labour and called for an ambulance, I went alone, as mother wasn't feeling too well. The midwives looked after me though. I was in slow labour for hours; I did not have any pain relief because I wanted to protect my baby, so I did it alone.

At last the baby was ready to come into the world, "push and breath, push and breath" they would say "push push go on your doing really well, ok one last push that's it come on push harder", and then, there she was born. I immediately named her Kelly Ann. They wrapped her up, and put her in my arms, she was born at 5:29 am, and weighed 5lb 6oz. It sounds a low weight but I was only small framed and weighed 7stone. I was then taken to the ward. I got chatting to other mothers.

One thing I couldn't understand is, that the midwives were acting really strange towards me. They kept on giving me more attention than anyone else. And one of them said "your going to be ok, you know that don't you?" she was crying. I was confused I didn't have a clue what she was going on about. I just replied, "yes I will be now I have got my daughter with me", and she cried even more, and left the room, "what the hell is going on" I thought. I fed my baby, put her on my chest, and lay on the bed.

Kelly woke me up shuffling around, so I got up and walked around the room with her "I love you so much Kelly", I would tell her. I went to the window to look outside. I couldn't believe it, I saw loads of police vans, cars and all sorts surrounding the hospital. "oh someone's in trouble" I thought. I sat back down on the bed, it was around 12:00 dinnertime. A midwife entered the room and sat besides me, and put her arm around me. "Whats going on outside" I asked. She blatantly said "she didn't know".

The next thing I know the social worker barges in with all these policemen, and told me to hand my baby over. "no not my baby" I screamed." your not taking my baby, no" I couldn't stop crying, as I screamed "not my baby no". A police woman came right up to me and said "I'm just doing as I'm told, I don't like this either," I screamed "why are you taking my baby? What have I done? I have done nothing wrong, your not taking her, "no" the police woman broke down, and whipped my baby from my arms. The other police held onto me while they left the room. Within seconds I was completely alone, I knelt down on the floor crying my eyes out, my heart completely broken and shattered. I just cried and cried and cried. I couldn't move off the floor, my whole body was just paralysed, I was having a nervous breakdown.

After about half an hour, my mother came in the room. She broke down crying with me and said "its happened to me too, Rosalyn I know how your feeling I know what your going through" with that she tried to lift me to my feet, but I felt as though my legs wasn't mine. Finally I stood up, with my eyes puffed up, and heart breaking, mother led me out of the hospital. We got into a taxi and crying my eyes out mother held onto me tightly all the way home just rocking me.

When we got home father immediately gave me some diazepam to help me to calm down, while mother got on the phone
and rang a solicitor for me I started to sleep downstairs with
mother and father, I was on the chair, dad was on the mattress,
mother was on the settee. I did not want to be on my own. The
solicitor came up to see me and I asked him why the social services took my baby from me, this is what he said "Rosalyn the
social services in their own sick way, believe that when a person
has been abused they will go on to abuse their own children."
My god I was sick to the stomach, "I would never harm my
child" I declared. He then went on to tell me that "I could have
a visit with Kelly for one hour" and that there was a court case
coming up in the family courts.

Father continually gave me diazepam to help me keep calm,
and if I'm honest it was properly them and god himself, that
stopped me from cracking up. I didn't sleep much at all, I would
just cry all the time, nobody could console me. Then the visit
with my daughter came. She was in a baby seat in the middle of
this small room at the NSPCC on her own. The social worker
asked me if I wanted a drink I said no. I hated the lot of them,
more so now. As I took Kelly from her chair, all the feelings of
her birth flooded back, and I tried not to cry in front of her,
even though she was just 6 weeks old I held her in my arms right
through the visit I had just 1 hour with her. If the visit went well
I could see her again. I hated saying goodbye to her and at this
point I could not hold back my emotions. I just walked home
numb from my head to my feet.

Week after week, I visited her, it was becoming so unbear-
able Then came the day of the court case, the social worker
straight away said "for the protection of the child, we want to
have Kelly adopted, and the visits to her birth parent terminated".

I couldn't believe what I was hearing. They said that Kelly was taken because, just as the solicitor said, the thought that, because I had been abused, I was going to go on to abuse my child." I would never hurt my daughter "I shouted" please just give me a chance to prove that to you, I've done nothing wrong" the social worker just ignored my cries and went on to say "Rosalyn is also still residing with the very people that abused her" I continued to shout "put me in a mother and baby unit then, please I don't care if it's a 100 miles away, I'll go," but they wasn't having any of it, I lost the fight for my beloved daughter.

The judge, though he could have had the last say, said "you never told this troubled young girl about your intentions to remove her baby from her, you have neither tried to support her or listen to what she has to say, I say this is abuse upon abuse, you have also wronged this young girl" with that he said "however the majority of the court is of the same opinion though none of you have even given her a chance, I have to rule with the majority of the court, simply because if anything should happen my neck would be on the line" then he said "you have literally washed your hands of this young lady and have done nothing to help or support her, you people are in the wrong" with that he shot out of the room." No you bastards, please let me have my baby, why are you doing this to me?, I want my baby, I need her, she needs me."

I just flopped to the floor and mother helped me up again, and took me home. Nobody, as I said, could console me. Two days later the social worker turned up and demanded that I sign the adoption papers, I completely refused. They went on to call me irresponsible, I grabbed the little table and threw it at her, and she soon left me alone. About now the prison where Brian was, had decided to give him early release due to good behaviour. We ended up back together.

Brian didn't allow me to use contraception, he didn't believe in it. I feared all the more that I was going to get pregnant again. He knew about what had happened to Kelly, but still insisted on sex without it. No to sex with him, was not an option. If I said no, he would beat me, I had bruises all on my arms, and on my back. My parents said they was getting sick of all the rows.

About 8 weeks later my worst fear was confirmed, I was pregnant again. This time however I had plotted a plan to run away, and use a false name. Brian said he didn't like the cuts on my arms, and made me put tattoos all over both arms; it looked terrible, I hated it. Mother went crazy with Brian, and said that "he didn't give a toss about me", I told mother and father of my plans to run away with this baby, scene as the social services refused to give me a chance to prove myself. They didn't know what to say, except "we will be here for you". Time went on and Brian got a job as an HGV driver, he was to off load at all sorts of areas even abroad. This to me was perfect for my plan. However my plan didn't work out, we was near Liverpool, when I felt a sudden rush of blood beneath me.

Brian rushed me to the nearest hospital; I was in really bad pain. The doctors gave me pain relief, and said they thought I was haemorrhaging. They went on to say I would need a cae-sarean section. I was scarred stiff. I was just 16 now. The doctors didn't have a clue at first who I was, as I was using a false name, and saying I was from Scotland. I forget the name I was using. "Ok its time" said the anaesthetist, there I was in serious pain, being wheeled down the corridor to the operating theatre's , I was just so petrified. Brian wasn't allowed in, and had to wait on the ward.

The doctors explained to me before hand, about the risks to

me and my baby, before they put me to sleep. They put the sleep medicine in my arm, and I was gone. I woke up on the ward in really bad pain, being pumped up on morphine. I forced my eyes open and shouted for a nurse, I asked her where my baby was, she told me "it was a girl and she had been taken to the special baby care unit". I tried to get of the bed as I looked down at the pad covering my stitches up, the cut spread from one end of my stomach to the other. The nurse put me in a wheel chair and took me to see my daughter, I called her Chrystal. She weighed just 1 pound 6oz, she was so tiny. I did all her cares, changing her, and I fed her the milk as instructed through a tube. "You're a great mother" said one of the staff. I was dying to tell her what the social services had done to me, but I didn't want to screw my identity up, "well, little did I know, they had already found out". They had identified me through the tattoos on my arms. I didn't know about this. I went up to visit her every day for 2 weeks.

One day I had to go home and get a change of clothing. I broke down and told mother everything, but she didn't seem to care, she just lay there, and didn't answer me, "I've given birth to Chrystal" I said "don't you care" she just stayed quiet, as did father. Father just asked if I wanted some diazepam before I went back, "yes" I said. With that I left with Brian and went back to the hospital. I got in the lift straight up to the special baby care unit.

When I entered I couldn't find Chrystal. I dropped all my clothes on the floor and crying, I ran frantically from room to room looking for her "where's my baby?, where's Chrystal"? The nurse took hold of me and took me to the parents room, she then explained how my real identity had been revealed, and the social services had taken her and she was moved to another hospital, by ambulance to Manchester "no,no,no,not again, oh god please not again" as I wept I went straight back to the social worker in Stockport, and grabbed her trying to get her attention, the bastards called the police out saying "I was being violent", I wasn't, I just wanted to know why they had done it to me again, and to tell me where my Chrystal was. But the police came and took me home. Mother and father didn't seem to care, they just totally went downhill, they were really depressed, but I had my own heartache and depression, and just couldn't help them.

I went on visits to Chrystal, and it was the same all over again, I lost the case. This time the judge had ordered them to pay out compensation to me, for what they had done. I didn't see a penny of it, till 10 years later. Brian still didn't leave me alone; I had started to hate him.

One night in bed he forced me to have sex with him, again and again, till I was torn inside out; I went to get two painkillers off father but he called me slag and said "stop fucking under my roof" I was shocked, I wanted to tell him, it was against my will, but I remembered what he did against my will too. I was not allowed to speak out. I went into the kitchen and got my painkillers, I also picked up the kitchen knife, I took the painkillers and hid the knife behind my back and went upstairs. Brian shouted "fucking hurry up" as I entered the bedroom he swung at me, asking what I had told my parents, "nothing I shouted" "keep your fucking voice down" he said, I pushed him off me, and swung the knife at him, but I missed. He pushed me to the floor and kicked me in the kidneys, all mother would shout was "stop your fucking banging you two" that was it I had enough. I told him to go or I was going to tell mother and father everything. He refused to go and belted me again, and raped me again.

The next day, even though I hated the social services, I sneaked off to see them; I was crying my eyes out, as I told them what Brian had done to me. They were literally the only ones I had left to turn to. They saw my bruises, and arranged for me to go to a women's hostel. There were lots of other battered women in there. I rang mother and explained to her what had happened, she immediately got father to kick him out. Father got on the phone to me and said how sorry he was, that be didn't know what was going on.

Whilst living at the hostel, I found out I was pregnant again, for a third time, I told the woman who looked after us all and also told her about the social services. She immediately informed them. The social worker came to see me, and said if I remain in the hostel, and don't have any contact with my parents what so ever, then there was a chance I could keep my third baby. I couldn't believe it, well of course I was going to comply with them; I wanted to keep my baby.

Each day I grew more and more excited. My bruises had started to heal, and I didn't feel as sore between my legs any more. I really got on with Jackie, who looked after us all. She used to sneak me food up to my room. The rooms were very empty, cold, and extremely boring. ITV was ok to watch though. Jackie also sneaked in a kitten for me, and some kitten food. I was 17 now. I loved that little ginger kitten. It was my only mate to chat too, especially when Jackie went off duty. The night times were the worst. So lonely, too much time to think I dreaded going out, in case Brian saw me. I got all my food needs off Jackie.

As time went on I got to about 8 months pregnant, I went out to nip to the shop, and nearly dropped dead when I saw Brian. With a typical battered woman's story, and a typical abusers apology, I ended up taking him back. "Stupid I know". I had to sneak him into the flat. He didn't touch me or hurt me, he stayed quiet.

One day, when I got to about 9 months pregnant, I wanted to see mother one last time to say a final goodbye. The both of them were acting really strange. They would say things like "if we ever died you keep the carpets and the kettle" I thought they were just joking around. Father hugged me really tight as I left, and so did mother, they couldn't have acted any stranger. Mother whispered "I love you Rosalyn, were both really sorry for what we have done to all our children" over and over they apologised, and warned Brian if he ever hurt me again they would kill him.

I left my parents house very worried, "something isn't right" I thought."They was not their usual self's at all". We got back to the flat, and that night I said to Brian "something isn't right with my parents, I need to ring them" but he talked me out of it saying, they would be ok. By now my little brother and sister was still with foster parents, my older sister Sarah was in a psychiatric unit, my twin brothers were living in their own flat in Wilmslow, and my older brother Daniel was living in Rochdale.

Two days later after my visit to my parents, Jackie asked me to come into the office She was holding a letter, she gave the letter to me and asked if I could open it in front of her, I said "no", I went back to my flat, and began to open the letter. A key suddenly fell out, "that's mother's key," I said. I opened the letter, the first line read "by now Rosalyn you will have gathered that me and your mother have had to end our lives" oh god no," I screamed, Brian was desperately trying to find out what was wrong with me, I couldn't tell him through the tears, I was too upset and choked up, I could barely even speak.

Heavily pregnant, I ran for the bus with Brian right behind me. I cried out loud all the way there, my legs were turning to jelly beneath me. I got to the gate of my parents house. "Please don't let it be true god, please don't let them be dead", I could hardly get the key in the door through the tears, I couldn't see a thing. I slowly turned the key, half expecting my parents to come and say it was all a misunderstanding. They didn't. Suddenly my whole body froze as I stepped into the hallway; Brian slammed tile door behind us and I jumped out of my skin.

The house was eerie and silent, apart from the two dogs that were running riot through the house. There was toilet roll everywhere, where the dogs had torn it up. I walked slowly through the hallway thinking that they would be asleep, perhaps in the living room, mother on the couch and father on his mattress, but no, as I entered the living room, they wasn't there. Father's bag was there and mothers handbag, all over the room, tablets were scattered everywhere. All the lights were out, everything was turned off. Also when I visited them two days before, the fridge was full of sterilised milk, and now the fridge was completely empty.

I turned to go back into the hallway, walking through, I stopped at the bottom of the stairs. I suddenly went ice cold I walked slowly up the stairs, sensing that my parents were there. And I was right. As I reached the top of the stairs, I peered over the landing, and there they were. Mother first and father collapsed over the top of mothers head, slumped over the top of each other. They had planned it all out very carefully. They both had a sheet underneath them, and a towel under their heads, and for some reason they only had a shirt and underwear on, half naked. Father's mouth was open with dried up blood coming from his mouth, and the same with mother. "mum and dad", "mum, dad" NO", I screamed, "no mum and dad, please don't do this to me, please wake up" I was frantic, completely heartbroken yet again, "mum and dad please please wake up, I am sorry I left you, oh please god help them" no, no, no , mum and dad please get up, I need you" frantically losing it and crying my eyes out, Brian went up to the side of them and felt their necks, he shook his head and said "I am sorry Rosalyn their dead".

I felt as though I was in a nightmare, like the continuing long nightmare chapter in my life, as I cried and cried my ribs ached, my world shattering around me, yet again. The whole world just seemed to stop in time. Unable to bear it any more, I went downstairs, halfway down, my legs went beneath me and I fell the rest of the way down, limping I went into the living room. I opened the letter again, barely able to see it through my puffed up eyes and tears, I read the next few lines. At the end of the letter they said to get an ambulance. The front of the letter had 2nd class stamp on it; they had carefully planned everything out.

As I tried to read on, I heard Brian explaining to the police and saying "their daughter has just found them dead, She is ok for now, he said, but she is heavily pregnant". It wasn't long before they tuned up; they cornered the road off from one end to the other. The police came, 2 ambulances and a coroners van. And the social workers. The CID also turned up. They couldn't get a word out of me, I could hardly even talk, I was cracking up. Brian told them everything. The ambulance men went straight upstairs. All I could hear from the landing was,"clear" beep, beep, beeeeeeeeeeeep, dead tone. And again, "clear" beep, beep, beeeeeeeeeeeep, dead tone again. The noise of the machine to try and revive them seemed to beep for ever, echoing with each long dead line. I ran upstairs pushing past the police who tried to restrain me. The ambulance men stood up and just said "I'm sorry" then made their way down the stairs. There was pink and white strips of paper with dead tones on them, all over the landing. The police tried to prize me away from my parent's side. I had my head on my mothers ice cold hand, crying "why mum and dad why"

I headed for yet another nervous breakdown. I just constantly cried as the picture of them remained in my mind how I found them. I went down stairs with the policeman and he led me to the other police officer, this is the one I knew when I was young, the one who knew the family. The police asked me if they could have my parent's letter, "no I cried, no you're not taking it, its all I have left of them". But they explained to me that I would get them back, they just needed to take them for examination. This other guy turned up wearing this white suit, he was picking the tablets up off the floor. "The coroner is ready" the policeman said to the others. The policeman that knew me said "now Rosalyn I want you to trust me now ok? I'm going to take you back to your flat and I need to ask you some questions". Brian didn't come with me, I am not sure where he disappeared to.

As the policeman led me out of the house, I could feel eyes everywhere, looking at me. All the nosey neighbours had come out to see what was going on. Although I saw them with my eyes, I didn't feel any of it was real, it was like I was in a nightmare, and was sure to wake up any minute now. But who was I kidding? I wasn't going to wake up from this never ending nightmare.

Back at the flat, the police tried to get as much information as possible out of me. The social worker also turned up and asked how I was, "well unless your blind love, I think you can see my parents just committed suicide, do I look alright dummy" what the bitch really wanted to know was, am I anywhere near giving birth yet. Brian turned up, and told me the family was waiting for me back at mum's house. The police said they was going to come back the next day. Brian took me back to the house, and waiting there was, Daniel, Philip, and Steve, all stood together in the living room. Philip and Steve decided to take on the removal of mothers stuff in the house, and they also had to beg the social services to fund the funeral. That night, back at the flat with Brian, I could sense an overwhelming feeling all round me, I went ice cold, and was positive I felt a touch on my shoulder.

All night I didn't sleep, I also had a letter that I had to pass on to granddad. Mother's father. "How on earth was I going to break the news to him" I thought. And what about, Mikey and Bethany? How are they going to be, and Sarah stuck in the psychiatric unit? Mother and father had written a letter to us all, and had left the responsibility of passing them on to everyone to me. Bethany's and Mikey's letter, I gave to the social worker. Philip, Steve and Daniels was attached to mine, and I showed it to them. With Sarah's letter I went up to the hospital and give it to her myself, this was in a space of 2 days. Then the police came up again an said "Rosalyn I am really sorry about this, but because you was the one who found your parents bodies, you have to be the one who identifies them too." I was devastated enough, without this.

Ready to give birth, I went to stepping hill hospital's morgue to formally identify them. I was led to this room that was all white and scarlet red. In front of me was two metal beds and mother was on one and father was on the other. Every emotion became raw again, I walked in between them, and the coroner said "don't touch the red blanket, an autopsy has just been done". I couldn't believe my ears. I was in complete shock, all over again, my heart began to break, I cried, I felt so weak. I walked in-between the two beds and looked upon my dead parents.

All I remember was seeing them lay there with their mouths

open and their hair scraped back where the coroner has had to wash it. And the colours of their faces was, white, purple, yellow, orange, where rigamortus had set in. Fathers hand was sticking out of the side of the blanket. I looked at the coroner and said "yes that's my mum and dad". I touched dad's ice cold hand, Suddenly Ii went dizzy, and collapsed. The next thing I know I was in hospital. This doctor came in and said "you're in labour my dear" and with that gave me an injection in my thigh. The room spun round, I couldn't talk properly, I could hardly move, I was lay on my side. Their voices seeming a million miles away. "What's going on? Why can't I wake up properly? What was in that injection the doctor just gave me? I don't want to push", I thought, "my baby isn't ready to come yet" I looked up, and I saw a drip attached to my arm, I tried to grab it ,"whats in it" I slowly gurgled out, the nurse told me that it was medicine to help induce my labour, "why?, my baby isn't ready to come" I could feel my eyes becoming rather heavy and found myself slipping in and out of consciousness. I could just barely hear one of them saying "shes really fighting it" fighting what? What were they talking about? Then as I struggled to keep awake, I felt another needle go into my thigh, I just knew this wasn't pain relief, I had pain relief before, and it was nothing like this. I don't remember anything after the injection.

The next thing I remembered was, being on a ward, and standing over my bed, a man dressed in black and white, he was a priest. What an earth was a priest doing here? I was still very dizzy, as I tried to get out of bed. I sat silent on the edge of the bed, as I looked down, my stomach almost flat "my baby, the one I'm going to keep, where's my baby" my cries became louder and louder, the priest came to my side and placed his arm round me,"the doctors are saying you had a nervous breakdown

Rosalyn, they took your baby away". My whole being failed to register what he had just said, I stood up and after collapsing twice, I managed to get to my feet, I strolled down the corridor, I felt like some sort of doped up mental patient. I stumbled straight into the back of one of the nurses, and fell to the ground. "Come on love she said, back to bed" "no." I said clinging to the little bit of strength I had, "I am going to find my baby" the nurse said "Rosalyn your baby is not here, the social services took her away" they said I could keep her", I said, "I did as I was told" the nurse said I was having a nervous breakdown, as it had only been days since I found my parents dead. "No I am ok, I can cope with my baby, I was only hanging on for her sake" with that I gave out a loud cry, now I really did feel like I was cracking up. Tear after tear, scream after scream, none of which sounded any where near as loud as the ones inside me." How can words ever be put into context how I was feeling, my whole world had literally been brought to an end.

Brian turned up, and said he was going away for a while, to get his head together. "What" that's all I could say I put my clothes on and went to leave the hospital, Brian was outside and said "you'll be fine you're a fighter" I shook my head and, walked off slowly, numb. Pain searing through my heart, my world shattered around me, I had nothing left, nobody left, nothing to live for any more, these are the words I repeated to myself as I walked to the via ducts in Stockport. This is where I will meet my end.

I crouched down on the bridge crying my eyes out, I just wanted to die. "I shouted really loud "I've got nobody left to live for, everything has been taken from me, I just want to die" with that I went to jump, suddenly I felt a hand grab my coat and pull me back,"get off me, leave me alone" I was being restrained by the police."How the hell did you know I was here?" I shouted to him, the policeman said, "dear Rosalyn this spot is notorious for suicides, the hospital told us what you had said before you left" then went on to say "I was one of them that saw your parents being taken out of the house, I know how you found them dead together, and I know that the authorities have taken all your children from you. I am here to tell you that your brother Daniel is living in Rochdale and wants you to go and live with him, I am also here to tell you that I feel moving to Rochdale would be a brand new start for you". I didn't want a brand new start, I wanted my babies back and my parents back, I had done nothing wrong, why was this happening to me? The policeman seemed quite upset and asked me to please come with him, "what do you care" I said. "I do care Rosalyn, you don't know me, but I remember you" where" I asked, "I saw you when you was very small, your father and your next door neighbour had a major argument, lots of police turned up, I was one of them, and you was trying to protect your father, you ran up to your neighbour and kicked him, I grabbed you then too, and gave you back to your mother, and here we are again years later." "Yes I said, but you can't take me back to my mother this time can you?" he stood me up and said "no, but I can take you to a family member that does care about you".

With that we got into his car and went to the police station, first we stopped at reddish police station to collect my parents belongings, it was my mothers wedding ring. I placed it on a chain around my neck, my eyes were really puffed up, as you can imagine, and I had a terrible headache. From there we went to Stockport police station. They made me a coffee and tried to cheer me up, but they couldn't. I told them that I would get to Daniel in Rochdale myself, and I was going to go back to my flat at brindale house. The police gave me a lift, and dropped me off. At first I just sat on the doorstep with my head in my hands, Jackie came out and she broke down crying with me "it's going to be ok Rosalyn, its going to be ok" she said ,as she comforted me.

As Jackie went back inside, I saw Brian walking up. "Oh god not him" I thought. "I am really sorry Rosalyn that I left you" feeling numb, all I could say was "ok". We both went back into the flat, the time would have been about 7-8 pm ,we both lay down and just slept and slept. We didn't awake till about 2:00 pm the next day. I was still just numb, still nothing felt real.

We stayed in the flat for about 5 days and a note was posted through the letterbox, it told me to contact the coroner. I went there and he told me that I had to go to my parents inquest and give evidence. "What the hell" have I not been through enough? But I had no choice I had to go.

Meanwhile little did I know that whilst I was preparing for the inquest, the social services were deciding the future of my last daughter who I had named "Angel" because she came into the world as my parents went out of it. I had received a letter from the social worker to say that "Angel was to be placed for immediate adoption, due to my mental state of mind." The bastards" I thought, they caused all this state of mind I was in. "Why didn't they just give me a chance to begin with, then tell me to leave my parents so they blamed themselves for it all, and ended up committing suicide as a result, and yet I still didn't get to keep my daughter, their excuse this time was "I was not in the right state of mind to take care of my child, and that I was cracking up".

I had not even seen Angel I didn't even know what she looked like. The day before the inquest Brian decided he was sexually frustrated, and once again had sex with me against my will, there he was on top of me, I just lay there numb, I couldn't move, I had no respect for myself anymore. He didn't just do it the once, he slapped me and said "you fucking move when I make love to you". I didn't move, I just stayed still and held onto my face. When he had finished the mental case, offered me a cup of coffee, "yes yes ok, I'll have one" I said in fear of being belted again. Of course the usual stuff came after like "I'm really sorry for hurting you, I'll never do it again I promise", crying false crocodile tears.

We just slept that night he didn't touch or hurt me. The next day was the day of the inquest. I put my jeans on and my top and, we got on the bus to the inquest. There was a woman sat besides me she appeared really nice and kept saying "you'll be fine just do your best" little did I know she was a reporter for the Stockport express. There I was in tears reliving my parent's death detail by detail, giving the best account as I could through the pain and devastation left behind. Then I had to sit through the coroner's report of the contents left in my parents stomachs and so on, and how their stomachs had burst due to the tablets, hence the reason for the blood coming out of their mouths when I found them. I sat as the coroner gave graphic details over from the autopsy he said they had been dead for three days. I felt sick to the stomach. All the time, I looked at this woman next to me, seeming to give me emotional support.

At last the inquest was over. The woman I looked up to, was as I said, a reporter. I could have killed her. Days later it was splashed all over the Stockport express. That was it, I had to get out. I went to granddads after previously giving him the letter, but he wasn't in. Brian went to work on night duty, I never got to go to my parents funeral, I got my stuff together and left

Brian a note, telling him I was leaving him. I got into a taxi, and left to go and live with my brother Daniel. I arrived at his house and he paid for the taxi.

My brother had become a Christian. He made me a bed up and we just talked till early hours of the morning, comforting each other. The next day Daniel introduced me to his church, Zion Baptist church. Everyone was great. Myself and Daniel used to have a laugh in church, as the minister tried to deliver his sermon. You know that feeling when you're not supposed to laugh and you do it all the more? Well that's what we were like, and my laugh was a long time coming. Daniel really helped me through those long lonely nights; he helped me to say a certain prayer. It went "our father who art in heaven, hallowed be thy name, thy kingdom come, thy will be done, on earth as it is in heaven, give us this day our daily bread, and forgive us our sins as we forgive those who sin against us, and lead us not into temptation, but deliver us from evil, for thine is the kingdom, the power and the glory, forever and ever, amen"..I loved this prayer, I would say it over an over again in my head. At church as I looked across the seats I saw a man staring back at me. Straight away something had clicked between us.

The next day was a Monday and Daniel had taken me to dovetails where he worked as a volunteer, the man I saw at church called Bill also worked there. I was talking to one of the volunteers in the office and I told her that I had missed my period, she told me to get a pregnancy test done. Now I was in Rochdale, I didn't seem to fear the social services. Although to my horror the test was positive.

The next time at church we was all having a cigarette outside, and Bill came unto me and said "if you like I can help you with the baby" with that we started a relationship. I really liked him; he came up to Daniels house and gave me a card and a box of chocolates. He was so different to the others I'd had. His motto was a Christian one "no sex before marriage." I was glad to hear this, but in a strange way I wasn't, I thought he didn't like my body, I was getting all these strange insecure feelings. I didn't understand it was because of the abuse and rape I had suffered.

One day Brian turned up at Daniels and put me up against the wall, but Daniel stuck up for me, I told him I had met someone else, someone who loved me for who I was. A couple from the church tried to explain to him too, but he got on his knees at Bill's house and displayed the usual rubbish, the false tears, the I will never do it again, but this time I was having none of it. And then he left. I was now becoming very close to Bill and had decided to move in with him. This however was against Christianity, but we knew that Jesus would understand due to my background. However our Christian brothers and sisters insisted that we get married.

I was 4 month pregnant, and one night I had really bad pain in my back and stomach. Bill took me to the hospital. Then upon arrival I started to bleed heavily and my waters broke. The nurses lay me down and said they could see the head of my baby; they helped me to deliver baby and placenta. Myself and Bill both knew there wasn't a chance the baby would survive. He was a baby, he had all his fingers and toes, eyes, body, the lot, no genitals yet though just a little tiny bump. So we said he must be a boy.

The nurses wrapped the tiny baby up in a dolls blanket, and gave him to us, we cried but at the same time we knew that he was with god now, and the authorities couldn't touch him. We held his body all night, and Bill took his cross and chain off and placed it around the baby's body. The nurses said "it was time to let go now" they explained that they had a little garden where they buried all the babies like ours; it was the baby memorial garden. Still bleeding quite heavily we made our way back home to Bill's.

We decided that we would get married and do it at Zion Baptist church. We prepared every day for it and had a wonderful amount of help from other Christian brothers and sisters. My brother Daniel was to be best man, and he looked great. Bill had a friend also called Bill who was x army. He said to Bill "don't watch her coming down the aisle." I was really annoyed about this.

Anyway here it was, my big day, I prayed to god that nothing would go wrong. As I entered the church the wedding music playing, I was so glad to see my little sister Bethany there, a smile lit up my face. My brother Daniel stayed with me and linked my arm down the aisle. This was to be the happiest day of my life. I was dressed in white and looked beautiful. Everybody was there. I felt a sudden rush of nerves flood my body and trembled really badly. As I got to the front of the church to Bill's side, the minister called Barry married us. I was shaking like crazy. I do, I said with a trembling voice. Bill said I do so confidently. There we was, Barry said "by the power invested in me, I now declare you husband and wife" and then came the music. We kissed each other and the first thing I said was "why didn't you look at me coming down the aisle" everybody laughed. Bethany came up to me and said how she saw my backside wobbling as I shook. I laughed; I was so pleased to see her, except she wasn't so little any more she was taller than me. It was a shame because she had to go.

Everybody tucked into the buffet supplied by the church. Myself and Bill went across the road to have our wedding photos taken. Bill was much older than me, I was 18 he was 42, but that didn't matter to me as long as you love one another. And we did.

Back home after the wedding and days later, things were going really well, until I started to open up to Bill about my past, opening up at the time wasn't a good idea at all. All my memories came flooding back and the pain. I had started to self harm again; my new husband Bill had a lot to take on. Over the weeks he had tried to stop me cutting myself, hiding glass and razors, my temper, my pain, he took the lot on, and supported me.

One night I had taken a serious overdose of aspirin and ended up in hospital for a couple of days after having my stomach pumped. My poor husband was about to bear the brunt end of years of pain, suffering, loss, pent up anger and emotions. He had to deal with everything as it happened. For the first year of marriage I was completely out of control, I hated everyone and everything, I didn't trust a soul. You would have thought I was possessed by an evil spirit or something, or maybe I was. For the first year of marriage at least, most of my pent up emotions came out. My husband just constantly supported me and refused to give up on me.

After a year of cutting and overdosing, I finally decided that it was time to face me past. I went to church and I gave my life to Jesus. We weren't living at the same address now we had moved to our own 2 bed house. I lost contact with Daniel, who had moved on himself. Things in my life however was about to take a rock bottom turn for the worst.

One night I had gone out to collect my prescription from the chemist, I was really deep into Christianity at this point. I saw a tall guy shivering in the cold, I asked him did he want my coat to keep warm, he said yes, I had ordered a taxi and he asked me if I could let him share it to get home. I had no idea he only lived a few doors down from me. So I let him share it. On the way home he asked me "are you rattling"? Rattling? What on earth was rattling, I thought he meant have I got tablets inside me. So I said yes thinking he was joking, at his house he invited me in for a coffee. "Ok" I said.

With my bible clutched in my hand I entered his home. I couldn't believe the stench, he said the rubbish bags hadn't been emptied, but no this wasn't that kind of smell. Well we got chatting, and what I failed to mention was that I was a weak Christian, still very screwed up. He asked me why I looked so down, I tried to tell him that I wasn't down I was just tired. I had gripping pain in my stomach too, I told him I had to go because of the pain. He offered me something for it, it was a green liquid, I had no idea what it was, even when he said it was methadone I had never heard of it before.

About 30 minuets after taking it I suddenly started to feel more cheerful and more confident. I left that night high as a kite. When I got home my husband said I looked better and more alive, he didn't know what I had just taken and neither did I tell him. The next day Boo he was called offered me some more but this time I had to pay for it. Boo he is dead now, apparently got battered to death. For three days I took methodone, then I started to fell ill, Boo said that my body was asking for something more now. He then introduced me to heroin. As he put the needle into my vein he said "this will make you feel much better" I didn't feel better, the pain in my legs stopped but I was constantly being sick.

Every day I had a bit more and having to pay for it. This had now been going on for weeks, I was completely hooked on heroin. I was a mess. The amount of heroin had increased, I ended up selling all my husband's tools and anything else I could get my hands on from home. I never stole from others though never. Weeks had passed and I had nothing left to sell, except one thing. There was nothing by now that my husband could do, only pray for my life. I ended up having to sell my body, I ended up a prostitute. I never dressed like the other girls. I always wore jeans and woolly jumpers.

After about 6 months of this I decided to go at it alone. I ended up using my own income to support my habit, although I always managed to maintain a steady £20 a day, or less. I had stopped the prostitution. I was on the heroin all in all about 2 years. After this time and my husband's endless pleas and the fact I had gone down to 6 stone in weight, I decided to kick the habit. I was supported by the church and received councilling and help from the drugs team.

The drugs team started me off on methadone then slowly decreased it, when I got to 5ml from 55ml over a two week period without heroin; they then placed me on the drug programme. The detox programme was murder, the cold turkey was horrendous but I wasn't giving up, I can do this I would say. Everybody supported me, I couldn't have asked for any greater help. But for me my ultimate help was the lord Jesus himself. I know it was him who really got me through it. Whilst detoxing I had contacted my sister again in the psychiatric unit, Sarah was so glad to hear from me, except Sarah wasn't Sarah any more, she was a different girl all together, as far as she was concerned the staff at the hospital was her family now.

Night after night I had to beat the temptation of heroin, the first 5 nights were the worst, but the detox drugs did help. "Fight it Rosalyn, fight it" every body would tell me. Days passed and Bill was a massive support but I believe Jesus was the

greatest. He I believe got me through the cold turkey, the sweat-
ing, the dioreah, the sleepless nights, the pain and illusions. The
detox programme was coming to an end. The drugs team took a
blood test from me They congratulated me for not touching any
heroin. I was so pleased with myself, something had finally gone
right for me. I stayed clean and beat the odds. "Well done Ros"
I would say to myself I thought, to go on heroin in the first place
was to hit rock bottom and you can't go any further down, and
now I am on my way back up I thought, and I was. I had now
been married 3 years+. I did my best in staying clean and going
to church and absorbing all the help I got.

For a whole year I really put my effort into doing the lord's
work. I had now been married 4 years. One day I made some
Christmas cards and put a little message from Jesus in all of
them. I took them into town and started to hand them out.
Some people were really nice, and others were just damn right
nasty, the ones that were nasty really hurt my feelings, I was all
alone in town. Tthen suddenly my husband showed up when I
was crying, he put his arm round me and led me home, "Ros
you did good, Jesus will be proud of you, don't let the rejection
get to you" Bill said. But the rejection did get to me, and all
night it ate me up within, about 7:00 pm I was feeling seriously
depressed, the rejection was eating me away. Bill was busy, I
went into the kitchen and pulled lots of tablets from the draw,
I laid them all out in front of me. "I must write everybody a
goodbye letter" I thought. I had written one to everyone I could
think of that would care. I was serious this time I am not going
back, I am definitely going to do it, I thought. I scooped a handful into my hand, I was just about to take them when I heard
"Rosalyn you'r pregnant, this baby you shall keep, I promise"
I heard this as clear as daylight, I am not in any way over exag-

gerating. I actually heard this voice loud and clear. "Can this be right" I thought looking at the calendar I could see I had missed my period. I put all the tablets back into the draw and ran in the living room and told Bill. He told me to take a pregnancy test the next day.

Well I did, I took 8 pregnancy tests each one a positive result. Oh my goodness I was over the moon. It had been 1 year since I touched heroin, and 3 years I think since I had self harmed. I was getting my life together. I had a midwife come to see me, she was a Jew, and she also said god will not let anyone take this baby from you. I was blooming, Bill took me away to torque when I was 5 months pregnant, and we really enjoyed ourselves. We was having a laugh as we chose babies names, Bill said "you deserve to be happy Ros and no one is going to take our baby". We decided on Isaac for a boy and Bethany I think it was for a girl.

One night I was laid in bed, I was 6 months+ pregnant when I felt a sudden gush beneath me. My waters had broken, I was rushed to the hospital and they tried to stop the baby coming, they managed to stop it for only a few days, then they said I had to be admitted to hope hospital in case the baby was born early. These brought back terrible memories for me of when my second daughter was born by caesarean section. I now became very paranoid. The midwives kept on trying to reassure me, but I wasn't having any of it, I didn't trust any one.

My labour had started and my husband arrived just in time, "Rosalyn open your legs the babies coming" oh no," no your going to take my baby" I sobbed, "We're not I promise you, just open your legs the head is coming" the midwife said. I finally opened my legs I had no choice. "Push Ros you can do it" my husband encouraged me" after a short while the baby came, "it's a boy" the midwife said.'well done sweetheart" my husband said. I cried my eyes out and told Bill to follow Isaac my son. Isaac was taken straight to the special baby care unit. I stayed with him constantly. Unfortunately Isaac had developed bowel problems and I was told he would be rushed to alderhey children's hospital. I went with him. When we arrived a doctor looked at Isaac while the staff got me a room to stay in. Bill was at home in Rochdale while I was in Liverpool on my own with Isaac. I refused to leave my son's side. He was only 2 lb 6oz when he was born, but I knew he was a little fighter. The doctor came to me and said "Mrs Kershaw I have some bad news, your son has developed a perforation in his bowel and will need an operation", poor Isaac, I thought, my poor son. I was told to go back to my room and I would be told when he was ready to go down to theater. I traipsed back and forth across the carpet, I rang Bill his dad, I waited. Then the phone in my room rang "ok Isaac is going down now". I then had to wait for the next call that he had come out.

I waited and waited and waited. Whilst waiting, a woman entered my room and said "Rosalyn I am the hospital social worker" I leapt off the bed and ran down the corridor, "you're not taking this one" I said. "No no Rosalyn come back, my aim is to keep you together, and you've been a great mother" she bellowed down the corridor. We sat down and I told her everything, she couldn't believe what the Stockport authorities had done. "I am going to try and keep you all together" she said. "Do you promise me" I said. She couldn't make promises but promised to write down all my good progress. Then I got the call "Mrs. Kershaw your son is back now on the baby care unit, the operation went well". I shot up to the baby unit, and peered into his incubator. I cried my eyes out and my face dropped when I saw my son's belly. He had a bit of his bowel bought out onto his stomach so it could heal. He had tubes all over him tubes up his nose and down his throat; he looked just like my second daughter did. The nurses asked me if I wanted to change him. I said ok, the nappy was the size of a tiny doll. I changed him and washed him, I was also taught how to change his little stomach bag. Bill visited occasionally, as he was suffering from a bad knee and had to travel from Rochdale to Liverpool so I understood, I however never left his side. Bill brought me a change of clothing plus there was a shop in the hospital.

One day I received a phone call from my solicitor, he said I had been compensated for what the authorities did and what my father did. The year was 2001 in the middle of August; I couldn't wait to receive the money. I didn't half treat myself, Bill and Isaac. I went mad with it. Isaac had started to get a little better and I was told he would be transferred to Liverpool women's hospital, also in Liverpool. When we got there Isaac again was checked on by the doctor while the staff showed me to my room.

After a week Isaac appeared to be doing well and we was told he would go back to hope hospital in Manchester. Isaac had started to do well, but then had another setback, after a while he was transferred after the observation of the doctors they thought it would be ok for Isaac to come back to Rochdale. So he came back. However this wasn't meant to be just yet, after another setback Isaac was transferred back to alderhey hospital. The doctors said they wanted to put Isaacs's bowel back into place which would require another operation. "Poor little boy" I thought. So into the theatre he went, when he came back to the ward he was very ill. He had a bandage going right the way across his little belly.

After days of intense care Isaac was once again on the road

to recovery. He definitely takes after me I thought, he truly is a fighter. Time went by and after going from place to place, Isaac was ready to come back to Rochdale. After a few days the social worker came up whilst Bill was there, and watched as we took care of our son. Isaac grew stronger and stronger; the reports on me were all glowing. The staff said "Isaac will be ready to come home soon." I shuddered with fear of what the social services would do.

A social worker rang the hospital and said that they had a meeting and decided to let me take my son home. I couldn't believe it, it was the happiest day of my entire life. I acted like a child, I ran up the corridor telling all the staff my great news, "oh my god, I cried, this time my tears was for joy, the doctor gave me vitamins and other medication to take home, and away we went. I felt so proud walking the pram down the corridor, though I half felt that it was all a trick and would be pounced on any second. But they didn't. When we got home a social worker was there and we hated this one. She was forever threatening us that she would take our son off us.

That's it we had enough we rang the head of social services, and asked for a change in social worker. Well we got one and we really liked her. Tina she was called. After being in touch for just 3 month, she said "we don't feel that you require a social worker any more, you're a really good mother and have more than proved yourself capable." Well I was over the moon with this. My life was finally coming together. I loved taking care of him. I became extremely protective of him as would any mother. I would of with my girls given the chance. Isaac was a very demanding baby, he demanded a feed on the hour, every hour, and I was really glad when he started to pile the weight on.

One day we decided to take Isaac to church. It wasn't Zion

though it was another church, called Silver Street. After much preparation and support we decided it was time to get our son baptised. Isaac looked so beautiful on his big day, he was dressed naturally in white, we all thanked god that Isaac had so bravely beat his early birth and dramatic bowel operation twice. We all stood at the front of the church and Isaac was in his father's arms, it brought me to tears I was so proud of my family .We did have godparents for Isaac, however I only wanted people in our son's life that we could trust 100%. However Isaac's godparents further down the months failed to do this.

We just thought that, if anything should happen to us that god himself would take care of our son and make sure he was well looked after. Bil'ls step mother was still alive, so she would have been an option of care if anything should happen to us, which it will not, I hope. I was also baptised at some point just before Isaac was born. Ok so there we all were on Isaac's big day. The day was videoed but I am not sure what's happened to it, a lot of things got broke as Isaac grew, he was an experimenter, he liked to take things apart. We had lots of photos done and what strikes me straight away about them is, just above Isaac's head there is a ray of light emerging from his head, only his nobody else's. I don't know, some would say it was light coming from the window, but I am not too sure, why was it only on Isaac's head and nobody else's??? Anyway that's up for debate.

Isaacs's day went very well. After speaking to the minister Ian White and a bit of fellowship with others myself and Bill made our way back home with Isaac. As Isaac grew a bit more, I decided to paint his bedroom, but not just any paint, oh no, this was permanent paint with a glossy effect, I painted balloons all over his wall, ABC letters and 123 numbers, Isaac loved it as he clapped his little hands together in approval. I just wanted to give Isaac everything I didn't have. I smothered him with love.

One day when a health visitor came I found myself having feelings I never had before. I didn't want the health visitor to touch Isaac; I started to become very paranoid that every one was out to hurt him. The health visitor tried to explain, it was because of my past, because everyone had hurt and abused me, I was now thinking they was going to do it to my son. Every time I took my son for a walk, I never enjoyed it, as I scowled at everyone. When someone came up to his pram I would begin to feel my temper rising. "Ok I thought its time to get a grip Ros, maybe talking about it or councilling." I had received councilling a while back but it wouldn't hurt to talk about it again. I didn't go for councilling instead I talked to my husband. He once again supported me and tried to get me to see that everyone wasn't out to hurt Isaac at all.

As time went on and with a course of anti-depressants I began to calm down and see things for what they really were, or did I???? When Isaac was one year old we decided it was time to move again.We came to Littlebourgh. We couldn't have moved at a worst time. It was in the middle of winter and the heating hadn't yet been switched on. So we all had to sleep in the freezing cold living room. Isaac was padded up in his baby rocker, Bill ended up with the settee whilst I ended up crunched up on a little chair. Because there was no carpet yet we used blankets to pad the floor out to stop Isaac hurting himself.

Well it took time but we finally got there. The guy came to put the heating on and we managed to get unpacked and all the rooms sorted out. We eventually got a carpet down when the social worker helped us out. We liked our new home after settling in. We had left all the bad memories behind us. Isaac had now begun to take his first steps, oh my, we were so proud of him, our little boy bad taken his first steps ,well done, good boy, we would say to him. Da da was his first words. When we had been there about 6 months.

My brothers Philip and Steve had come to visit. I hadn't seen them in a long time. They had to deal with our parent's death alone. I didn't know how it was affecting them. They still clung on to the abuse they suffered at the hands of our mother. They were also about to find out they were uncles to Isaac. Philip and Steve had also done really well to get used to what had happened to them and to our parents. They dealt with the funeral and the removal of our parents stuff from the house. They loved Isaac and promised to be good uncles to him, and never let him down.

Isaac had begun to walk really well, however my motherly instincts had suggested that something wasn't right with him. I had discussed this with Jenny our new health visitor. She suggested we keep an eye on things until he's a little older. Jenny is great, the best health visitor and friend we ever had. When Isaac was one and a half, we sent him to a nursery school. The teachers didn't pick up on anything wrong straight away, but I did. Each time he went to nursery I would notice something different in him. I noticed that he was much more behind the other children and after a time so did the teachers.

Back home I was talking to my husband about it, and for some reason it suddenly dawned on me half way through the conversation that I had missed my period. I told Bill and he wondered why the conversation had suddenly changed. I went to the chemist after dropping Isaac off at nursery and bought 4 pregnancy tests. I went to the bathroom and did all 4 of them. All four was positive. Oh boy I was over the moon, I ran downstairs and told Bill, he was over the moon too. When I picked

Isaac up, I told all the teachers too, they were really happy for us. Some work had begun with Isaac to determine how far behind the other children he was. And just as I suspected Isaac had substantial understanding and speech and learning difficulties. It was also determined that whilst he was one and a half years old he was only a few months old in his mind. All this was because of his very early birth. But we coped with him, we all pulled together to help him and we made sure that everyone knew what the other was doing.

He had started to go to speech and language therapy and also saw the follow up doctor at Liverpool who wanted to see him till he was five, but there was no way we could keep traveling to Liverpool. Time went on and Isaac started to show positive signs of coming on, but still very behind. I was about 36 weeks pregnant and my waters broke. Once again the hospital tried to prevent it but they couldn't. I was sent to hope hospital again. This time it wasn't so bad because the birth was a lot further on than Isaac's. I asked the doctor why I kept on having early births, and he said I had a short cervix and weak pelvic walls. Bill couldn't be there this time as he had to take care of Isaac. However I had this one midwife that absolutely refused to leave my side. She was ready to go off duty and still did not leave me. I was in labour all in all about 36–38 hours.

As any mother will know, the pain grew more and more intense. I lay on my side and pushed and pushed. After a while, "it's a boy" they wrapped him up and put him on my chest but had to take him to the special baby care unit. "What are you going to call him?" said the midwife, "Jordan" I said. Jordan only spent a couple of weeks in hospital, one in hope and one in Rochdale. Then he came home. It took us quite a while to get Isaac used to his new brother. Isaac's nursery was about to change all its hours round and would of only had one hour there so we didn't see the point as it was two miles there on the bus and by the time I had dropped him off I would have to collect him again, so he stopped going. This gave Isaac more time to get used to Jordan.

Jordan was quite a good baby he only cried 3 times I think in the night for his food and slept the rest. As Jordan grew we noticed that he too started to have speech difficulties though not as bad as Isaac's. By now Isaac was two and a half and Jordan was one and a bit and walking. Jordan's first words were daddy. Well again time went on, birthdays went by, and Christmas went by.

One night myself and my husband, after putting the kids to bed, had a discussion about trying for one last child to complete the family. I wish we never did. We was both found to be infertile and had to embark on a course of IVF. It was a terrible mistake. The hospital took my eggs and my husband's sperm and three of them fertilised. I was brought back to the hospital to have the eggs put into my uterus. After a few days I had a pregnancy test done.

We all waited eagerly for the phone call to come. Ring ring, it was here. "Hello" they said, "Mrs. Kershaw your pregnancy test was positive" oh thank you I said all that pain hadn't gone to waste". Little did I know the pain and anguish that was about to follow. When I got to 4 weeks pregnant I started to feel agonising pain in my stomach. I took painkillers for about a week more. The agony grew 10 times worse. My brother Philip came up, he said "that's it I am getting you to the hospital."

We got as far as the front gate when I suddenly went white and almost collapsed. Philip rushed me to the hospital. At first the hospital thought it was constipation, when suddenly I had a rush of blood beneath me, the nurses and doctors rushed in and said "you've had a miscarriage, however we also suspect your having an ectopic pregnancy too "I couldn't believe what I was bearing. I had a miscarriage and now was being wheeled down to theatre for a suspected ectopic pregnancy. There I was in serious bad pain; the doctor gave me the medicine to put me to sleep.

When I came round the doctor said "you're lucky to be alive, you bled heavily internally after your ectopic pregnancy ruptured, that's why your stomach was so swollen, it was blood, also because it had ruptured we had to remove your fallopian tube. I had stitches from one end of my stomach to the other, it reminded me of the caesarean section I had with Chrystal my second daughter. Well that was it for me; my body couldn't take any more. I was placed on pain killers and I am still on them now as I have extensive internal scarring that is very painful.

My doctor is really nice and very understanding. We had decided after all this that we should move on again this time to a 3 bed house. We needed a 3 bed because Isaac and Jordan were fighting so bad we was desperate to split them up, we ended up putting 2 years rent up in advance in desperation. The year now is 2006 and Jordan is almost 3 and Isaac is almost 5, Isaac still has extensive problems but is getting a lot of support, Jordan's speech is also coming on, they are two wonderful children, typical tantrum toddlers, but good boys.

I am still a Christian although I do not go to church right now, and myself and my husband have now been married for 9 years. We have excellent support from our health visitor Jenny, she has been there for us for a long while now and I trust her 100%. At times I think without Jenny Koulourie, I would of become very depressed.

Jordan is in nursery and Isaac has been at a special school

for some months and is doing so well. I have also been appealing to abused women and children in the local newspaper to come forward and speak out. And hopefully I'll move on to work with those who self harm, but first I'll go to college.

There is no one more experienced than the one who has experienced all these things at first hand. As for the future???? Who knows what the future holds for any of us, except god himself. What I can say is "LIVE EVERY DAY AS IF IT WAS YOUR LAST" ENJOY LIFE THE BEST YOU CAN, AND NEVER TAKE ANYTHING FOR GRANTED"

Thank you for reading my biography I hope it has helped someone else. God bless you all, and I hope life treats you all well.

Nightmere!!

When I was five I used to play
When I was six I was sunshine's ray
When I was seven things turned bad
When I was eight my parents went mad!! !!

When I was five I would play with my dolly
When I was six I' pretend to be molly
When I was seven the bruises would start
When I was eight my daddy broke my heart! ! !!

When I was five I was a princess or queen
When I was six on my daddy I would lean
When I was seven my legs got blue
When I was eight my daddy showed me something new!!!!

When I was five I would dress in pink
When I was six I am beautiful I would think
When I was seven I was in so much pain
When I was eight my daddy raped me again! !!!

ISBN 142510333-2

9 781425 103330